How To Outsmart Your Kids

Merry Christmas!
Love,
Dorrin and Rebecca
1993

How To Outsmart Your Kids

The Parents' Guide to Dirty Tricks

by Bill Dodds

Illustrations by Mark Engblom

Meadowbrook Press
Distributed by Simon & Schuster
New York

Library of Congress Cataloging-in-Publication Data

Dodds, Bill.
    How to outsmart your kids: the parents' guide to dirty
    tricks / by Bill Dodds.
        p.   cm.
    Rev. ed. of: The parents' guide to dirty tricks. ©1989.
    1. Child rearing—Humor.   2. Revenge—Humor.
    3. Parents—Psychology—Humor.   4. Parent and child—
    Humor. I. Dodds, Bill. The parents' guide to dirty tricks.
    II. Title.
    PN6231.C315D62   1992
    818'.5402—dc20   92-40981
                                                      CIP

    ISBN 0-88166-196-1

Simon & Schuster Order # 0-671-86978-7

Editor: Bruce Lansky
Editorial Coordinator: Elizabeth H. Weiss
Production Coordinator: Matthew Thurber
Desktop Publishing Coordinator: Jon C. Wright
Cover Art: Stephen Carpenter
Illustrations: Mark Engblom

Published by Meadowbrook Press, 18318 Minnetonka
Boulevard, Deephaven, MN 55391.

BOOK TRADE DISTRIBUTION by Simon & Schuster, a division
of Simon and Schuster, Inc., 1230 Avenue of the Americas, New
York, NY 10020.

96 95 94 93   6 5 4 3 2

Printed in the United States of America

For Tom, Carrie, and Andy

(But you guys can forget about the $100 I promised each of you if you stayed quiet while I worked on this book. Next time get it in writing. I'm only doing this for your own good. To teach you a lesson. It's not the money. Honest.)

Contents

Introduction: Fighting Fire with Fire ix

Bondage and Discipline 1

Food 9

The Doctor and Dentist 16

Love and. . . Gender 24

Birthday Parties 30

The Holidays 37

Going Out 44

School 51

After School 60

Go to Bed! 66

Sibling Rivalry, Civil War 74

Fighting Fire with Fire

No doubt you've already discovered that parenthood is a wonderfully fulfilling experience, except for the part where you have to come into contact with your children.

It doesn't need to be that way. We wrote this book to help you cultivate the attitudes, approaches, and bloodcurdling screams that can make being a parent so much easier.

Who Are "We"?

Who is this "we" offering advice? We are Bill Dodds and we are a parent. Like you, we have the basic urge to ensure the continuation of the human race. And we have a primal drive for personal survival. So, like you, we have become a classic, raving schizophrenic as we deal with the realities of everyday parenthood. That's why we are first-person plural. That's why we are nuts.

That Doesn't Sound Right

You might disagree with some of the suggestions in *How To Outsmart Your Kids*. That's all right. We had many long, heated arguments which went deep into the night and kept the neighbors up until they finally called the cops, before we settled on what you'll read here.

If you come across something that seems particularly inaccurate, offensive, or stupid, then it's probably something you should be using very often on your child.

Chapter One

A good parent can yell louder than any kid.

Bondage and Discipline

As a parent, you have to rely on discipline to survive your years of bondage. Remember, raising a child is not like taking your life savings—all you have and all you will ever have—and stuffing it down the nearest sewer drain. It's not nearly that easy. Or rewarding.

Everything you have belongs to that little one; not only your money, but your time, sanity, and bathroom. In other words, you're a slave to your child.

But enough about bondage. We include it in this first chapter only because you wouldn't read one called *Discipline*. But by combining discipline with *bondage*, we can appeal to your kinky

1

tendencies and snooker you into examining these simple but effective ways of making your child toe the line.

Wagons, Ho!

Think of parenthood as a heavy, wooden cart with square wheels. Lucky for you there's a sturdy team of oxen to pull the load: **Fear** and **Guilt**.

Any time you discipline your child, ask yourself these two questions:

1. Does my action make my child fear me?

2. Does my action make my child feel like dirt?

Begin at the Beginning

We strongly recommend that you begin disciplining your child before he or she is born. Remember, if a preborn can hear music, a preborn can hear criticism. If you think you're pregnant, rub your tummy and say,

- "Sit up straight!"

- "Get that thumb out of your mouth!"

- "Quit kicking!"

If you think your wife is pregnant, help her out with these:

- "Listen to your mother!"

- "Shape up!"

- "Come on, whatsa matter with you, huh?"

The Line

After your child is born, this statement will automatically pop into your head:

"I'm only doing this for your own good. This is going to hurt me a lot more than it hurts you."

It's kind of a hormonal thing, whether you're the mom or dad. The beauty of this line is that not only do you come to believe it, but your child feels bad for you every time you punish him or her. But this line works only, ONLY, if you say it without laughing. Practice in front of the bathroom mirror and remember how well your parents used it. Thanks to them you shouldn't have any trouble. See? They really *were* doing it for your own good.

A Shot in the Dark

An effective guilt tactic is to suddenly yell out **"I see you!"** when your children are in a different room.

It really keeps them off balance.

A Short History of Discipline

1910—"I'm sorry, Obadiah, but we are sorely disappointed with you. You may not watch the fireplace tonight."

1936—"You've been a naughty girl, Eleanor. No radio for you."

1961—"You're in the doghouse, Kenny. No TV."

Today—"Gosh, Jason (Joshua, Jeremy), we are so emotionally drained because of the choices you've made. It's good to think of others, to empathize, before selecting an action involving consequences that will impact not only yourself but those in your immediate environment with whom you interface."

See the problem?

Try: "You're busted, Ace! No television, VCR, video games, computer time, or jawing on the YAK-TEEN line. You have stepped in **deep doodoo!**"

Give it a shot. See if it doesn't work an eensy bit better.

Cigarette? Blindfold?

You can have a lot more fun tightening the old thumbscrews if you let your children select their punishment. They know they have to think of something beefy or you'll take back your offer and decide for them.

This is when it really helps to have a laugh that sounds like Vincent Price on Michael Jackson's *Thriller* album.

"So, my little miscreant," you say, and give a V.P. laugh, "what will it be?"

Laugh again.

Making Allowances

Some parents insist on giving their kids allowances. Maybe you've fallen into this trap. Not sure it's really a problem? Try this simple quiz:

1. Does your four-year-old have more cash than you do?

2. Does he have a nicer stereo?

3. Do you owe him more than $20?

4. Do you wish you were four years old?

Don't worry. Here's what you do:

1. Double his allowance.

2. Then find an excuse for punishing him and taking it away.

Positive Reinforcement

Positive reinforcement means different things to different people. The experts in child rearing (those who make pots of money writing books about kids so they can afford to have nannies take care of theirs) say it means rewarding good behavior.

This may be a problem for you because you've never actually witnessed good behavior from your child.

To most parents, those in the trenches with Play-Doh under their fingernails, it means backing the other parent. **Always** do this. For example:

Mom: Jimmy, you are wrong, bad, way out of line, and headed for the electric chair.

Dad: Yeah.

It's important that you're able to talk about both kinds of positive reinforcement. It comes up a lot at parties when parents get together. Usually the speakers are referring to the experts' def-

4

inition, not the real definition. It is your job to talk knowledgeably about the experts' definition. Then you can go home and yell at your kids.

All parents do.

Don't feel bad about this. Remember, a good parent is one who can yell louder than the kids.

Take a Break

The same experts who recommend that you give your kids an M&M, some Cheerios, a CD player, or a Porsche if they do something good also insist that you must not punish them while you're angry.

This is a serious problem. You, like all parents, have been angry since your child was born. You must say to yourself and your child, "I am not angry, but **boy!** am I peeved. With a capital P."

You may also be "miffed."

A Slight Modification

The technique the pros recommend **can** be adapted to really stick it to your kids.

Good news, huh?

Let's say you've doused the fire and put the cat out of its misery and you turn to the little cherub who is responsible. You now:

1. Stare coldly for several minutes.

2. Say, "I am too angry to talk to you right now."

3. Walk slowly from the room and go to the kitchen.

4. Take out all of the pots and pans from the drawer under the oven and bang them around with great vigor.

You don't need to actually punish the child. There's nothing you could come up with that will match what he's imagining.

But that's good! Children today need better imaginations.

"Time of Sentencing
Set for Later This Afternoon"

Don't forget to take advantage of the old standby, "Wait until your father gets home!"

(Again, we must mention the value of laughing like Vincent Price.)

Of course, this can be modified: "Wait until your mother gets home."

And if your spouse happens to be away on a business trip, it helps to jot down a little reminder to talk about the problem when he or she returns. Something like **"Tell What Susan Did!"** written in bright red paint across her bedroom door works quite nicely.

The Proper Response

Maybe you're afraid you'll overreact to things your child does. This is nearly impossible. You have every reason to fear you'll underreact. Always keep in mind the basic philosophy practiced by storm-trooper police officers in crime-infested metropolitan areas:

- If the bad guy makes a fist, pull out your nightstick.

- If he pulls a knife, pull out your gun.

- If he pulls out a gun, activate a nuclear device.

And so on.

To Everything There Is a Reason

Be wary when your child goes into a "stall" pattern and asks why she has to be punished so severely for **only** putting her little brother through the family's new, big-screen TV set.

Anytime your child asks "Why?" you must immediately reply:

1. "Because I said so."

2. "Because I'm bigger than you."

This is called *dialoguing* with your child. It's the hottest thing since positive reinforcement.

Don't Punish Your Child
with Something You Want Him to Do

Here we step into the very dangerous mine field known as *reverse psychology*. If you punish your kid by making him do something you really want him to do, then whenever he does it, he'll think of it as a punishment.

Huh?

If you send your son to bed a half-hour early for something he did wrong, he'll always think of going to bed as a punishment and will fight it every time.

Here's what you should say: "You have been a holy, living terror this evening. You have to stay up and watch a rerun of 'Death Valley Days' on the tube."

He will plead, "No, Mama! No, Daddy! I'll be good."

But you must **be firm!**

Yes, You Must Be Firm!

You must never

- give in,
- back down,
- flinch,
- blink, or
- breathe

when disciplining your children or **they will walk all over you.**

In their new soccer cleats.

Think of yourself as a loan officer. And think of your kids as loan applicants.

Punishment and Age: A Little Test

Here's a little test to make sure you're punishing your children at the correct PAL (punishment age level):

1. Your three-month-old wakes you up in the middle of the night and has the gall to want something to eat.

2. Your six-year-old uses his crayons and your living room wall to prove he can spell very well if the words have only four letters.

3. Your seventh-grader has not stopped whining for the last 72 hours because Brenda said Rob said Marty said she (your seventh-grader) wasn't so cool and he (Marty) also said her new sweater looked kinda dorky.

4. The Alabama Highway Patrol caught your 17-year-old son speeding.

Now, what is the appropriate response for each situation?

a. say "No, no!" and really mean it

b. take away the car keys

c. heat up a can of Spaghettios

d. make the child snip the phone line

The answer in all cases is b. There is no greater punishment than taking away the car keys, even if your child will not be old enough to drive for another 16 years.

The Good Book

By now you may be saying, "Does all this mean that big book on raising kids is worthless?"

Not at all.

Be very careful not to set a beer bottle on it or use it to prop up one corner of the sofa. That book is an ideal gift for a couple with a newborn. Isn't that how it ended up in your home?

That title has been in 49.5 million American households. Isn't that impressive? Especially when you consider that only 17 copies were actually printed.

Wrap it up and pass it on.

Chapter Two

Children can be cruel, which makes revenge that much sweeter.

Food

How do you get your children to avoid fatty, greasy, disgusting, unhealthy food?

Don't let them eat from your plate.

But that's not enough. You need to help them develop an attitude that respects the human body and recognizes the importance of a nutritious diet.

You need to make sure they don't end up like you.

A Quick Refresher Course on Nutrition

To find out if your child is eating right, you have to start by asking the tough questions:

9

- "You don't look like you're eating right. Are you?"

- "You call that breakfast?"

- "Who ate my Oreos?"

Then you have to learn about good food and good nutrition. Here's all you need to know:

- Ice cream, milk, and cottage cheese come from a cow.

- Bran is important because without it there'd be nothing but raisins in your cereal box.

- Apples, bananas, pears, and peaches will rot before they're eaten.

- A nutritious source of protein that is not in the red-meat category is peanut butter and jelly.

Now that you know all this, you're ready to learn how to feed your children.

How to Burp the Baby

It doesn't matter if you breast-feed or bottle-feed your infant. After finishing her meal, your little one will snuggle up on your shoulder and throw up down your neck.

This is called burping the baby.

A baby will always miss the cheap, old-diaper burp rag and let go on your best blouse or shirt. There's something instinctive about hitting the most expensive piece of cloth around.

The solution is to use a silk burp rag and wear clothes made of old diapers.

Weaning the Child

Some parents worry about the correct age at which to wean a child. Don't be concerned. Mom will find out when the baby has sprouted teeth. She'll let Dad know with the universal signal, "Get it off me!" Then she'll pull the little pit bull from her bosom and shake and shudder like Humphrey Bogart in the leech scene from *The African Queen*.

Dad doesn't need to worry about this.

It will be as natural and pleasant as delivering the baby was.

Red Goop, Yellow Goop, and Brown Goop

Some people say baby food looks like it has already been chewed once. That, of course, is ridiculous. It looks like somebody has sucked on it for a year and a half and chewed it twice. Your job is to get it from a tiny jar into a tiny mouth.

The easiest way to convince your child to eat is to make mealtime a little game. Try playing

- Choo-choo train: "Open the tunnel!"

- Airplane: "Open the hangar!"

- Angry, tired parent with a baby in the house: **"Open your yap and eat this!"**

In general, feeding Baby her goop takes about 10 hours. When you're in a rush, here's how to save time:

1. Open the jar.

2. Smear one third on your baby's face.

3. Smear one third on your good pants.

4. Plop one third on the floor.

Learning Patience

If by some miracle you get some of the goop into the baby's mouth, she'll spit it back on you and **laugh.**

It does no good to scold her. She's just having fun.

Instead, take some photos of her making such a big, fat **pig** of herself and save them to show to her date when he picks her up for the senior prom.

Give 'Em the Chair

One of the wisest investments you can make is a sturdy high chair. Any device that straps a kid down during mealtime is a boon to parents. Of course, you can't keep your child in there forever. He should be released when he

- needs to go to the bathroom
- has eaten all the vegetables on his plate and your plate
- is leaving for college

Sugar in the Morning, Sugar in the Evening

Maybe you're one of those parents who think a child won't develop a taste for sweets if she never eats anything with sugar in it.

This is your first baby, isn't it?

You also think your little one will be nonviolent.

And you'll be terribly hurt when she enters kindergarten and is called into the principal's office for beating the snot out of a classmate who didn't hand over his Snickers bar.

All children love sweets. Use this to your advantage. Here are some examples of classic bribes:

- "Timmy, you may have a cupcake for dessert if you drink all your milk."
- "Sharon, you may have a cookie if you loan me $20."
- "Allen, you may have an ice-cream cone if you drop the gun."

Make It Look Like Junk

The best and easiest way to get your children to eat food that's good for them is by making it sound like a terrible, life-destroying treat:

- "OK, who wants some McLima beans?"
- "How about trying some Kentucky Fried Squash? Extra crispy!"

But How Do You Tell?

How do you tell if a product is good for your child? Let's take breakfast cereal. In general, if it's shaped like little ice-cream cones, dinosaurs, cookies, or cheese Danish, it's not the best thing for them.

Also, check the list of ingredients. If the first three are "sugar, corn syrup, and high-fructose concentrate," you know it's for adults only. Hide it way in the back of your cupboard behind the bales of shredded wheat.

Washing Up for Dinner

Don't ever make the mistake of telling your children, "Go wash up for dinner," and expect them to go wash up for dinner.

Get real.

Instead, say:

> "Go into the bathroom and don't fight over who gets to go first and turn on the water, hot water, in the sink and put your hands—both hands, both sides—under the water and take the bar of soap and rub the soap on your hands—both hands, both sides—and then put the soap back down in the soap dish and hold your hands—both hands, both sides—under the water and then turn the water off and reach around and get a towel and dry your hands—both hands, both sides—until all the water is gone and then hang the towel back on the towel rack and come and sit at the table."

Memorize it. They won't.

The Vegetarian

Maybe you have a teen-age son or daughter who has become a vegetarian and is making mealtime a living hell for you and the rest of the carnivores.

Relax.

Order a large pepperoni pizza.

That'll end that nonsense.

Snack Time

Two to five minutes after your child has eaten a large meal he or she will begin foraging through the cupboards for a snack.

Keep a bowl of wax fruit on the kitchen counter and tell your kid, "First, eat a banana. If you don't want a banana, you aren't that hungry."

You could have real fruit, but it would rot in the bowl before anyone touched it.

The wax fruit bowl is especially handy if your child walks into the kitchen after dinner and you've just crammed three snickerdoodles in your mouth.

Don't try to say anything; just point at the fruit.

The TV Game Plan

You can always use television to get your child to eat. Don't forget that a child will eat anything—anything—as long as the TV set is on.

You could put beets—no kidding, pickled beets—on your kid's plate and he'd shovel them right in without taking his eyes off some old "Three's Company" rerun.

How to Pack a School Lunch

Getting your child to eat what you pack in a brown bag isn't as difficult as many parents believe, as long as you understand that no matter what you pack, your child will eat only cookies and Cheetos. He won't even look in the sack. He'll sniff it and pull out anything with sugar or salt. The rest goes straight into the lunch room dumpster.

You can save yourself a lot of time in the morning if you pack cookies, Cheetos, wadded up newspaper, and a few rocks.

Your child will become suspicious if you don't comment on his lunch. Once in a while ask,

- "Did you eat all the crust of that seven-grain bread I used for your sandwich?"
- "You still like liverwurst, don't you?"
- "Did the other kids tease you about the prunes?"

He's not going to starve. The quarter you gave him for milk plus the two dollars he took from your wallet while you were out in the backyard in your pajamas picking up rocks will buy him french fries and a milk shake.

K. P.

It's easier to get your kids to help clean up after dinner if you make up a duty roster like the army does. Let's say you have three children. You divide the tasks into three groups: 1. clear the table and put away the leftovers; 2. rinse and put the dishes in the dishwasher; and 3. take the dishes out of the dishwasher and put them away. You assign a specific task to each child and rotate on a three-day basis. That way, every night each child will have something new to moan about:

- "I hate clearing and putting away!"

- "I hate rinsing and stacking the dishwasher!"

- "I hate emptying the dishwasher and putting the dishes away!"

What could be more fair?

Fighting Cholesterol

Children can be cruel. Just as you're about to enjoy a nice breakfast of bacon and eggs, your child may smile, say "Cholesterol!" grab at his chest, and fall over pretending to die.

You can't do much right then. Wait until he's snarfing down a couple of chocolate bars, then say, "Pimple!" and put a brown paper bag over your head.

Dining Out

Eating out can be a lot of fun for the whole family if parents and children eat at separate tables.

Or at separate restaurants.

Or in separate states.

The little ones feel so grown-up when they get to sit by themselves. Especially at the end of the meal when the waitress drops off the bill, and they discover Dad has said, "Separate checks."

Chapter Three

If your child is properly wired, you'll never have to call a TV repairman.

The Doctor and Dentist

Part of your job as a parent is convincing your child it's more than OK, it's really a lot of fun, to get stabbed in the rear end with a needle or wear orthodontic headgear that looks like a UHF loop antenna. Part of your job is dealing with the doctor and the dentist.

How Do I Know if My Child Is Sick?

Here's the rule of thumb: Your child is really sick if you want to take the day off work and watch something on television.

And, its corollary: Your child is faking it if you really have to go to work. In that case, she only has the "sniffles."

What Are the "Sniffles"?

A sniffle is a pesky little bother that sometimes makes your youngster reach for a tissue.

It may be accompanied by an extremely high fever and the spontaneous release of a variety of body fluids in a most unpleasant manner, but your job as a parent is to say, "You just have the sniffles, honey. You can go to school. Don't be a wienie."

Checking the Old Thermometer

The thermometer is your best friend. If your child complains of a scratchy throat, a bit of a cough, and large, oozing pustules covering most of her body, you simply reach for the thermometer.

"No," you say, after she has sucked on it for an hour and a half, "No fever."

The real beauty of this ploy is that if your child is faking it, she'll feel guilty because there's scientific proof that she's a lying piece of scum. If she does have a fever, she'll think it didn't show up because, uh oh, she let the thermometer slip out from under her tongue.

That's why you must always say, "Keep this under your tongue, honey. I'll time it. Three minutes." Give or take.

For a Really Good Time

It's especially entertaining if your little one has a stuffed-up nose. Watch her try to breathe through her mouth and keep that poison-filled vial tucked properly under her tongue.

Parenting does have its moments.

How Do You Read Those Things?

It's a well-known fact that a child can't read a thermometer. The truth is no one can. Just twirl it a little bit and say, "Normal, see?" and hand it to your kid.

Where Is It?

Children often counter your tactics by breaking the thermometer when you're not around and flicking the mercury into your Mr. Coffee.

No problem. Dig around in the back of the medicine cabinet and pull out the old "baby" thermometer. Carefully explain how this particular model is not used orally.

Watch as your child's face crinkles in disgust and suddenly, she's **all better!**

But What if Your Child Really Has a Fever?

Never forget that your child will stick his face near bare light bulbs, hold it under a scalding Shower Massage, and bury it for hours in an electric blanket cranked up to China syndrome just to get a reading on the thermometer above 98.6.

So, how can you tell?

1. Have the child lie down, face up.

2. Place a crayon on his forehead.

3. Then watch to see if it melts completely.

If a chunk of crayon remains, call him a fake, a liar, and a poor excuse for a human being and send him to school.

If nothing is left of the crayon but a puddle and wrapper, admit that he has the sniffles and remind him he doesn't want to be a wienie.

In either case, tell him to go wash his face.

A Medical Emergency

Sooner or later, and perhaps very often, your child will have a medical emergency. This is not a term to bandy about. Remember, it is **not** a real emergency unless:

- It happens in the middle of the night.
- You have to get gas on the way to the emergency room.
- The closest parking space to the hospital is a half mile away in a neighborhood that wouldn't feel safe to a demented urban-guerrilla terrorist.
- The nurse-medic-practitioner-barber can't see you for at least three hours.

- You and your little one must sit next to a gunshot victim who is slowly bleeding his mind-altering-drug-ridden blood all over your shoes.

- Your medical insurance doesn't cover this particular problem.

So don't talk about a "medical emergency" if it's merely a compound fracture with a protruding bone, a life-threatening illness, or a chainsaw mishap.

If it **is** a medical emergency, rush your child to the airport and take the first flight to England or Sweden or some other country with socialized medicine.

You'll be saving yourself a lot of time and trouble.

Choosing a Doctor

Don't worry about choosing a physician. You'll never see your child's doctor. (Just as, in the delivery room, you never saw your obstetrician, Dr. Icedigits. No, it was some intern—a kid named Skippy—who helped out there.)

So keep in mind that you don't choose a doctor, you choose a waiting room.

Choose carefully. Ask yourself:

- Is the room brightly lit and pleasantly furnished?

- Is there an assortment of toys for my child to play with?

- Are other children waiting to see this physician?

If you answer "yes" to any of these, this is not the place for you.

Brightly lit, pleasant surroundings cost money. And who cares what the joint looks like if kids are crawling all over it, drooling and sneezing and germing up a bunch of toys your child wants to stick in his mouth?

Yuck.

Use your head.

Holistic Medicine

Yes, use your head because a lot of illness isn't really illness; the patient is just a little bit nuts. That's why a holistic approach is so effective.

For example, the best way to fight a sore throat is to take three pounds of mentholated lard and slather it on your child's neck. Then pin an old tube sock around it. Make him wear the sock for five minutes or so and ask if he feels better now.

Or serve your daughter that disgusting slop known as milk toast. Be sure to mention that your grandma called it "graveyard stew."

Sound Advice

It is your obligation to provide sound advice for your child after she has hurt herself. If she crawls into the living room and says, "I fell off my bike and landed on the curb and I think I just shattered my hipbone," it's your job to say, "Well, don't do that again."

Some parents, those with a keen sense of humor, might substitute, "Do it again. I didn't see it." Your child will chuckle heartily and forget about the pain that was making her writhe all over the floor.

The Universal Antidote

No matter what the medical problem, you can fix it with a kiss or a plastic bandage.

Stick with the kiss. It's free.

Do not buy bandages with cartoon characters on them. They aren't worth it. No child has kept a bandage on for more than 90 seconds. Within a minute and a half your child will be back for another one unless, when putting on the first one, you say, "Don't take this off. And for heaven's sake, don't peek under it."

Of course she will peek, ruining the bandage, but now she can't tell you she did.

An Earache

You should know that your child has an earache. Right now. Even as you read these lines.

There was a time, quite a while ago now, when for almost three days he *didn't* have one. But don't plan on seeing such a time again.

All children have earaches all the time.

Your child takes a bubble-gum-flavored prescription medicine called Amoxicillin. Give it to him every eight hours from the moment he's conceived him until he's eligible for a gold watch and full pension.

Don't miss one time or your child may have to get **tubes.**

Those are your only choices. Either your child gets tubes or remains an Amoxicillin junkie.

In a pinch you can drop 17 chunks of Bazooka Joe into your blender and hold down the frappé button for 15 seconds. Have your tyke drink it while it's still frothy.

He won't know the difference.

Use a sugarless bubblegum if you're concerned about cavities.

"Ourfriendthedentist"

Do you know what a cavity really is? You may think of it as a bunch of sugary crud that has eaten away at the enamel of your child's tooth and is now munching on a dainty nerve end.

Ha!

It's a tiny hole that will take many, many dollars to fill. And it's going to get bigger unless you go see "ourfriendthedentist."

Always say it as one word. You may come to believe it's true. Your child never will. The best way to convince him to visit the dentist is to be honest. (The exception that proves the rule.) Tell him you have chosen a health-care professional who costs 50 percent more than any other dentist because he gives his young patients dime-store toys worth about three cents each. Retail.

Brush, Brush, Brush

If you brush your children's teeth from the time they are very young, they'll quickly learn that they don't have to do it themselves and will quit.

It's easy to get them to resume the habit once they get a little older and galloping hormones take possession of their bodies. Suddenly your son will be interested in girls. That's an ideal time for you to say, "So the young ladies today really like a fellow with furry teeth, huh?"

Metal Mouth

It costs a lot, a ton, megabucks, to provide your daughter with braces. But she knows that. That's why she whines, groans, cries, and says she hopes you suffer a painful, lingering death very soon.

There's one way to make her gasp and fall silent.

Say **"adjustment."**

Such as, "I think it's about time to go back to the orthodontist for a slight **adjustment.**"

Or, "Dr. Lockingpliers said you need to see him about an **adjustment** as soon as you've stopped screaming from the pain of metal strands pulling at your teeth."

Or, "Move that TV antenna around a little bit, will you? Something is wrong with the **adjustment.**"

Wired to Receive Radio Free Europe

If your child is really being a baby about having her teeth shifted around inside her mouth, ask your orthodontist to weld together an RFE (Radio Free Europe) appliance. The pros call devices like this an *appliance* because to a kid it feels like a toaster oven has exploded in her mouth. After a month or two of coat hangers protruding from her mouth and a strap across the back of her head made from the waistband of a pair of Hanes all-cotton briefs, your daughter won't mind having "only" braces.

Just a Bite

Maybe your child doesn't need braces, just a "bite." This, as we all know, is a fake mouth roof with some silver wires around the edges.

Children take great delight in removing their bite at the dinner table and leaving it where the dog can eat it. You can impolitely laugh at how funny your kid sounds with a "bite lisp," but that hardly compensates for having to buy a new one every three or four days.

It's much more practical to take two red poker chips and one white one (to make the proper pink color) and a couple of paper clips and bake them in a muffin tin at 325° Fahrenheit for 20 minutes. (Allow a little more baking time at higher elevations.) You can do a dozen at a shot.

But at Least You've Got Your Health

Always remember it is *very* important that you keep your child in tip-top shape. Then, when she says, "My life stinks! No fair! I hate you!" you can reply, "At least you've got your health."

Chapter Four

At this time in your child's development everything will remind him of sex.

Love and...Gender

Sooner or later you're going to have to sit down with your child and talk about...you know. There's nothing to be ashamed of. "You know..." is a natural part of life. After all, none of us would have been born if it weren't for...you know.

It doesn't help to put it off. Just ask your own parents. They plan on having that talk with you any day now.

Speaking of your mom, isn't that her right over there watching you check out this chapter on sex?

Ha ha!

Made you look!

How to Avoid
Telling Your Child About Sex

- Let him watch the soaps.

- Let him watch TV commercials for perfume, beer, blue jeans, or all-season steel-belted radial tires.

- Let him pick out VCR movies at the rental shop.

- Let him go to school and talk to anyone over three years old.

- If you are a more traditional parent, use the time-honored method of keeping farm animals in your backyard.

You can avoid a lot of embarrassment if you remember your job is to answer **only** the question that was asked.

Child: Where do babies come from?

You: The hospital.

If you prefer a classical smoke screen, try this:

Child: What is sex?

You: It's Latin for "six."

Mother Nature's Time Bomb

These tactics may work well, but they will not work for very long. That's because there is a gland inside your child called the pituitary. This is Mother Nature's time bomb. Even as you snuggle up next to your newborn, it is ticking. There's nothing you can do to stop it.

That's why, from the time your child turns 11 or so, it's very wise to wear a heavy, metal combat helmet. Your little baby is about to turn into a **sex machine.**

When that happens your home will explode. Your neighbors will come running over and say, "We were hoping it was only a gas main, but it looks like it was Mr. Pituitary."

Think of puberty as nuclear holocaust.

And keep that helmet strap fastened tight.

The Warning Signs

If you watch your child carefully, you may be able to detect the early signs that indicate a change is about to take place.

Don't blink or you'll miss them.

The only outward signs are a widening of the eyes and a tiny smile that says, "Oh, I get it!"

One moment your kid is a normal, relatively-happy youngster who hates the opposite sex and all forms of mushy stuff. The next moment he or she acts like the type of person your mother warned you to stay away from.

In the Classroom

To help you the school system has developed a course in sex education that your child will have to take at this time.

You must encourage your child to read all the literature provided and study hard. The theory here is that your child will confuse sex with homework and decide it is very boring.

Sometimes this works. For a while.

It's easy to determine if, and how much, your child knows about sex. While you and your child are watching reruns of "Cheers" and "Night Court," see what happens.

- You laugh at something and your child says, "I don't get it." (Pray this happens.)

- You laugh at something and your child laughs, too, and neither one of you says anything because you're both kind of embarrassed the other is in the room and neither can believe the other person really understood the joke.

- Your child laughs at something and you say, "I don't get it." (Pray this doesn't happen.)

The Eye of the Beholder

At this point in your child's development, every word, gesture, vegetable, and national monument will remind him of sex. He will constantly burst out laughing, roll his eyes, and nudge his best friend, and the two of them will giggle uncontrollably.

You can counter with "That's not funny. That's the Lincoln Memorial."

It won't work.

Do **not** admit that, hey, you know, when you look at it from this angle....

Make a Sharp U-Turn

At this point in your parenting you must contradict all the earlier messages you gave your child. You know, how you said sex is wonderful and not something bad and they'll understand it someday and it will all make sense when they get a little older.

Well, they **are** a little older and now you have to **constantly** remind them that sex is

- evil

- vile

If you don't do this, they'll reach adulthood with a healthy attitude toward sex. This is **not normal**. You, of course, want your child to be normal. It's up to you to make sure he or she feels the same way every other human being felt approaching adulthood: confused, frightened, and guilty.

At the Movies

A lot has changed with sex in the movies over the past 50 years. We mean on the screen. It wasn't very long ago that Clark Gable rocked the country when he took off his shirt while not wearing an undershirt and said "damn." (As movie buffs will recall, the exact line was: "Oh, damn, I forgot my undershirt.")

Today the movie industry provides a rating system that prepares you, the parent, for what your child will want to see:

G—"I'm not going to that."

PG—"That's just for little kids."

PG-13—"I guess that one's OK."

R-17—"Who cares? It'll be out on video in six months."

X—"We decided not to go to a movie. We were at the mall. Don't you trust me?"

How, then, do you get your son or daughter to see a wholesome family show?

Supposing you can find one, do **not** mention the rating and become very vague about the title. But be sure to say you're pretty certain the word "leather" or "chainsaw" or "stud" is in there somewhere. For example:

- *Leather Bambi*

- *The Sound of Chainsaw Music*

- *The Absent-Minded Professor Stud*

A Common Mistake

You must take great care to avoid confusing sex with the name of a band. If your son wears a T-shirt that says, "SEX! SEX! SEX! LUST! YOUR BODY NOW! SEX!" he is only indicating his preference in music.

This is called Heavy Metal.

We gave you a little test earlier in this chapter. Remember when we were talking about Mr. Pituitary and how you need to wear a helmet? A **heavy, metal** helmet?

As a parent, it's your job to respond immediately every time you hear the words "heavy" and "metal." The correct response is "I think you would really like the Everly Brothers if you just gave them half a chance."

A Little Help

Fortunately, advertisers realize what a difficult time this is for you and your child, so they thoughtfully sell your kid posters, bumper stickers, skateboards, record albums, tapes, and countless other items dripping with sex.

Don't be such a prude.

Remember how your mom and dad hated it when Elvis shook his hips or the Beatles tossed their hair around? Well, you sound just like your folks when you say you don't like that lead singer who screams about going to the prom with a corpse and then, as part of the act, bites the head off a rat.

Loosen up.

It helps a lot, **a lot,** to imagine what your grandchildren are going to spring on your kids.

Does That Really Help?

It not only helps to imagine the unsolvable problems your child will face as a parent, it might even make some of them happen.

Remember how much your dad hated boys with long hair and girls with jangling jewelry?

Now look at your son with two earrings in one lobe, and your daughter who combs her hair with a Bic disposable razor.

It's no coincidence.

Chapter Five

Drive the kids to the video arcade and give them four quarters. Then lock those doors!

Birthday Parties

Once a year your child is allowed to go wacko, destroy your home, drive you nutsy cuckoo, **and** have a cake with candles on it. The cake is what makes it different from any other day. It's his birthday, that annual hell with more sequels than *Nightmare on Elm Street.*

And you have to buy presents and invite other little kids over to eat too much and upchuck on your living room carpet.

Baby's First Birthday

You have two choices the first year.

1. Bake a cake, which your child will smash, and buy expensive gifts, which he'll break, lose, or throw at you.

2. Skip it.

Baby's Second Birthday

See above.

Baby's Third Birthday

Welcome to the house of the doomed. By this time one of your child's little playmates has had a birthday party and your kid was an eyewitness. We advise you to tell your child she can have a party on her birthday.

Then tell her she was born on February 29.

The Theme Party

The party will be easier on you if you choose a theme.

"Happy Birthday" is a very poor choice.

"State Pen" is a very good choice.

At a "Happy Birthday" party all the little children ruin their best clothes, inhale a beautiful cake it took you an entire day to make, run through your house breaking the two or three items your child somehow has failed to break, and flush little plastic party favors down your toilet.

At a "State Pen" party all the little children dress in cheap coveralls, eat bread and water, and are handcuffed at all times.

Outside the Home

You will soon discover the advantage of holding your child's birthday party at

- the local skating rink
- a pizza parlor
- a movie theater
- a padded cell

The beauty of having the party outside your home is that you can take all the children inside a public facility and then go sit in your car and listen to the radio for a couple hours.

Remember to lock those doors!

That's Entertainment

A large part of your time will be spent providing entertainment. It's your job to organize games. The children will want to play

- "Cat in the Microwave"

- "Is It Safety Glass?"

- "I Can Scream Louder than You Can"

You'll live longer if you can make them play

- "Here's a Dollar, Sit Down"

- "Here's a Dollar, Shut Up"

- "Let Me Call You a Cab"

Food, Glorious Food

There's no need for you to serve a variety of favorite party foods. Do yourself a favor and just pick up a couple crates of sugar cubes.

Don't forget the candles.

Capture It on Film

If your child is still pretty young, take photographs of her ripping the wrapping paper off those expensive gifts you bought her. Then say, "Let me get those out of your way so you can enjoy your brown-sugar/corn-syrup/cotton-candy cake." Put the gifts in the trunk of your car and return them to the store the next day.

If she asks about them later, scold her for having lost all those nice presents.

Already.

Tell her she won't be getting so many next year since she didn't take care of them.

Look hurt.

After the pictures are developed, give her a set to remind her what a generous parent you are.

Is That All There Is?

No matter how much you spend on gifts, your little one is going to rip open the packages as fast as he can and then whine, "Is that all?"

Be nice and wrap a **lot** of packages.

It's not necessary to put anything inside them.

Boxes

Every parent discovers that children like the box more than the gift. Use your head. Give your child a box. If he likes sports, make it one a basketball came in. If he likes music, make it one that held a radio. If he's the intellectual type and you're already nagging him to get into the right college, give him one that had a computer in it.

The Perfect Gift

If you must—guilt, guilt, guilt—buy a birthday gift for your child, remember that the ideal present is big, heavy, secondhand, and cheap.

An old washing machine is perfect.

(It's true your child would like a washing machine **box** even better, but it won't last as long.)

A Suggestion

Often a family member or a parent of one of your child's friends will ask what your child would like for her birthday. There is one very good answer—cash.

Don't accept a check unless it's made out in your name and the person shows you two forms of ID.

Batteries Not Included

Any toy your child receives will need batteries. These will not be included because they cost twice as much as the toy itself.

There are three types of batteries:

1. Regular (cheap). These die halfway home from the store.

2. Alkaline (very expensive). These die when you walk in the door.

3. Rechargeable (extremely expensive). These cost a fortune, need a recharger, and are lost down in the sofa before you can say, "Well, look again. They didn't just get up and walk away by themselves."

The solution is to always keep a set of dead batteries on hand. That way the new toy will never make those obnoxious noises that so delight your child.

A Favorite Aunt

If your child has a favorite aunt or uncle or a goody-two-shoes godparent, he may get a toy **with** the batteries. If this is a **very loud** toy, the batteries will last a long, long time unless you sneak into your child's room at night, snatch it, turn it on, and put it in the freezer until breakfast.

The Slumber Party

Your child might be invited to a birthday-slumber party. Do **not** stop and ask yourself, "What kind of a crackpot adult would spend that much time with all those children?" Remember that **this is a good deal.** Another parent will be taking care of your child and a dozen other screaming peewees all night long.

But it's not a perfect deal because later you will be expected to host a slumber party for your child. If you're stupid enough to agree to this, you'll soon notice that it isn't really a party and there's no slumber.

No, this is a VCR-movie/gossip/pig-out marathon.

Even if you hold the party on the spring night when all the clocks are turned forward an hour for the beginning of daylight savings, you'll still be stuck in a house with several thousand children for eternity.

So agree that your child may attend a friend's slumber party *only* on the condition that her friend's parents adopt her.

Instant Wallflower

If you don't want to hold a party for your child, make sure she doesn't get invited to a lot of other parties. Have her give one of the following gifts to her little friends:

- socks

- an atlas

- tasteful stationery

- any of the disappointing gifts your grandmother gave to you (Aren't they in a box out in the garage somewhere? Or in your mom's basement?)

Going Out

Maybe you're afraid you'll feel bad if you don't do **something** for your son's birthday. All right. Ask him if he'd like to eat dinner out. Have him call up some of his friends and see if he can get himself invited over.

The Name Game

An ordinary paper napkin costs about half a cent. A birthday napkin costs about a dime. A birthday napkin that has your child's name printed on it costs more than your first car.

Next time you're in the card shop, check out the discount table and grab whatever package of name napkins is there. It's a lot cheaper to use these and legally change your child's name to match them.

How to Break a Toy

Your parents and brothers and sisters may be giving your child toys that make a **lot** of noise to get even with you for being such a peach when you were growing up.

You can solve this problem by learning how to break a toy. Here's how:

1. Say, "Let me see that, honey."

2. Snap it in two or cram a large piece of birthday cake into the mechanism.

3. Apologize profusely and promise to fix it right after the party.

4. Toss it on top of the refrigerator where your kid won't see it until she's five feet or taller.

Contact a Lawyer

Very few new parents know this, so please take note: in every state of this great union of ours, it is a **criminal** offense for a member of the extended family to give your child

- a drum

- an ant farm

- a puppy

It is **not** a crime for your spouse to give your child one of these items, but you **may** legally shoot him or her. Well, not really, but no jury in the world would convict you.

Chapter Six

How to throw a real scare into your neighbors.

The Holidays

Your life (some life, huh?) as a parent is made more difficult by the fact that at least once or twice a week there is a holiday. This is the commonly accepted abbreviation for "holler all day."

A New Year's Day Check

On the first day of the year your child will wake you up very early and ask, "Can I have the corn chips and bean dip that are all over the sofa, and who's that guy sleeping on the kitchen counter?"

Isn't it great the way your child comes up with the same questions you used to ask your mom and dad after their New Year's Eve parties? Here's how to handle this one:

1. Say, "Get me my checkbook."

2. Say, "I'm writing out a check for one thousand dollars. It's yours if you let me sleep another 10 hours."

3. Make a mental note to call your bank first thing January 2 and stop payment on the check.

Do not give your child your automated teller machine card.

Firm Resolve

On New Year's Day you are supposed to do some resolving. Please realize this has **nothing** to do with being a parent. You cannot "re-solve" anything about being a mother or father because you have not solved anything yet.

Taking Down the Everbrown

Many families take down their Christmas tree on New Year's Day. Your child may be feeling a little blue about the holiday season coming to an end. It's up to you to help him get his mind on something else. Try, "Don't forget you have **school** tomorrow!" or "Didn't you say something two weeks ago about having **homework!**"

Something New for the Calendar

Dr. Martin Luther King, Jr., Day is celebrated in mid-January. This is a new one. So new, in fact, that your kids won't be yammering for you to buy them something. Within the next 50 years this day will be commercialized just like other holidays and parents will be expected to shell out dough for something worthless and in poor taste. But, and here's the good news, your children will be grown by then, and you'll be dead.

So enjoy the day.

Roses Are Red

The big holiday in February is St. Valentine's Day. During the first two weeks of the month the newspapers are filled with ads for skimpy underwear and expensive chocolate.

Buy your spouse one or the other. If you buy both, you could have problems. Maybe you've never noticed, but a federal law requires that all Valentine's Day ads include a drawing of Cupid—that little baby with the bow and arrow. He's there to remind you what skimpy underwear and expensive chocolate can lead to.

On this day your child is expected to bring several thousand tiny cards to the other children in his or her class. After your son or daughter is in bed on Valentine's Day eve, pull the cards from their envelopes and rewrite some of the verses, just for fun. Here are some fine examples:

- "A new hairdo, Valentine! You look like a poodle."

- "I saw you, Valentine. And I'm telling."

- "You're breaking the leash law, Valentine."

- "Give me your milk money, Valentine, or I'll break your legs during recess."

See if that doesn't make your child's holiday a little more exciting.

Remembering Our Leaders

George Washington and Abraham Lincoln were born in February. So were Babe Ruth and Jimmy Durante, but your child's school doesn't care diddly about The Babe or The Schnozz because it doesn't have several million film strips on them like it does on the presidents. Viewing those film strips is a very important part of your child's education because it kills a lot of class time. We mention this only because for each film strip your child has to do a project.

So try to look really impressed with your child's scrapbook titled "My good buddy, Chester A. Arthur."

You can honestly say

- "That's the finest tribute to Chester A. Arthur I have ever seen."

- "You really did an excellent job pasting down those pictures."

- "Who the hell was Chester A. Arthur?"

By Gosh and By Gory!

Did you know that any little boy or girl not wearing green on St. Patrick's Day will be pinched by all the other children?

The Annual Easter Battle

At Easter time your child wants to snarf down chocolate bunnies. You want her to eat colored hard-boiled eggs.

Need we say more?

Do yourself a favor. For the same results,

1. Take a bottle of food coloring and splatter your kitchen and yourself.

2. Eat egg salad sandwiches for a week after Easter or until you are sick of egg salad.

3. Give your kid the candy.

The Annual Hunt

Before you collapse from the cholesterol in all those egg-salad sandwiches, tell your child that instead of hiding gum drops or jelly beans, you've hidden silver dollars that are hers to keep if she finds them.

Tell her you hid them **outside.** Far away outside.

Enjoy the quiet. It will probably be several hours before your child thinks, "Where would my mom (or dad) get silver dollars? Where would my mom (or dad) get a **dollar?"**

The Fourth of July

On the Fourth of July, American parents sip cold drinks and say, "Wouldn't it be wonderful to be independent?"

This is a great holiday if your employer provides good medical coverage for your entire family. You'll need it. Here are some of the dangerous things your child will want to do:

• Set off explosives under you when you're not looking.

• Shoot flaming torches onto your roof.

- Hold a slender wire showering sparks all over you, himself, and your plastic lawn furniture. He'll wave this flare—not quite as cool as a welder's torch—and then drop the burned-out wire in the grass where you'll later impale your bare foot with it or send it slicing into your spouse's eyeball the next time you mow the lawn.

At this time remind him:

- Most of those objects are illegal.

- You **never** did anything like that when you were a child.

- He should stay out of that bag of stuff you and your neighbor bought across the state line.

You'd better not use the second item if your parents or a brother or sister are at your home on the Fourth. They'll laugh so hard they'll inhale an ice cube, you'll have to call the medics who might report your personal arsenal to the cops, and then you'll end up in the pokey.

Labor Day

This is a three-day weekend, the official end of summer. You are supposed to take a break from your daily labor by working your buns off getting all the junk done around the house you've been avoiding the past three months.

Labor Day is a glorious holiday because your child will be going back to school the next day. It would have been called Independence Day, but that name was already taken.

Your child may have a few butterflies in his stomach about starting another school year. It's your job to reassure him. When you tuck him into bed that night, say things like

- "Maybe the guy who mashed your face every day last year moved away."

- "I'm not packing lunches this year. You're going to have to eat cafeteria food."

- "The fifth grade won't be that tough. Everything is easier the second time around."

- "I'll just bet you're not the only kid who didn't grow a single inch over the summer."

Halloween

Halloween is the day your child pesters the neighbors for a snack instead of bothering you. If you really want your kid to scare the other folks on the block, have him dress up in a three-piece, polyester suit and say things like, "Why don't we sit down at your kitchen table and review the coverage you already have? My company has a policy that will better suit your needs. When is your birthday? Here, have a pocket comb or rain bonnet."

Tell him nothing is more frightening than a life insurance salesman. The neighbors will throw bags of candy at him to get him off their porches.

All those treats must be inspected by you because of ugly rumors that a depraved lunatic-psycho is putting things in candy.

Do your best to perpetuate this rumor; it gives you first crack at all the loot. Isn't it amazing how all the chocolate bars are suspect? Mommy and Daddy will take care of disposing them.

Remind your child that a depraved lunatic-psycho **never** tampers with those little boxes of raisins.

Veteran's Day

If your child is over 12 years old or very large, this might be an excellent time to see if you can get him or her to enlist in the Marine Corps. Play up the part about **free,** real cool camouflage clothing.

Thanksgiving

Choose one:

1. Spend all day in the kitchen preparing a turkey, potatoes, dressing, fancy vegetable, a cranberry dish, rolls, and pumpkin pie. Spend three minutes at the table. Spend all night doing the dishes.

2. Hand your child a box of Ritz crackers and a jar of Cheez-Whiz and say, "Don't eat too much. You'll spoil your dinner."

Fun with Santa

A big treat for you this time of year is taking your child to see Santa. Just look at your little one screaming with terror as he struggles to get away from that strange old man with the long, white beard.

Get a picture of that.

Heck, get a nice frame, too.

Helping Your Child Become a Hypocrite

Maybe you've been tempted to perpetuate the Santa myth long after your child has learned there isn't any Santa, only VISA and MasterCard.

You can put a lot of pressure on her by saying, "If you're too old to believe in Santa then you're too old for gifts."

DO IT!

She'll say she believes just so she gets something.

There's an important lesson here for your child: some things in life come your way only if you lie your brains out.

Some of the best things in life.

Chapter Seven

When the monsoon arrives, use your car phone to call for help.

Going Out

It's only natural that you, like all parents, eventually say, "LET ME OUT!" This would be a wonderful plan if you didn't have to take your children with you.

But you do.

The Eight-Cylinder Rocker

If your child is very young, your destination doesn't matter. All that matters is that you strap her into the car seat and head out.

She will immediately fall asleep.

That's why cars were invented. Sleeping children kept falling off horses.

This is another amazing baby fact all parents soon discover. An infant will be screaming her widdoo wungs out—and shattering your widdoo eardrums and nerves—and nothing you do will make her fall asleep.

Except a ride in the car. (The same is true for a ninth-grader in algebra class.)

To get the most out of this maneuver, don't use an imported car with flow-through ventilation and a smooth ride. Use a '64 Chevy with windows that can't roll down and a heater—always stuck on "high"—that can turn an old-fashioned Coke bottle into a puddle.

A Mobile Home

The saddest part of this dearly loved trick is that your child wakes up as soon as you get home and open the car door.

The advantage of the Chevy over the sardine-sized import becomes apparent when you realize you'll be living in that car until your child is in kindergarten.

It's not as bad as it sounds.

At least your baby won't wake up.

If you have a car phone, you can order pizza.

Faking It

If you insist on leaving the car, you can try to convince your child she is still in the vehicle by shaking her gently and making traffic sounds, like: "chugga-chugga," "beep-beep," "red light," and "get out of the way, you freaking idiot, before I run over your head!"

Assigned Positions

If your children are a little older, they won't sleep in the car. Your problems begin before they even get inside. Every child wants to sit in the front seat. Every child wants to sit by a window. No child wants to sit in the middle of the back seat.

They are convinced there is no place worse than the middle of the back seat. Until they take a good, long look in the trunk and you explain how the little light goes out once the lid is **slammed shut!**

(Don't mention the roof rack and elastic straps. You'll only be shooting yourself in the foot.)

"I Was First"

A favorite game of all children is to race to the car and be the first to touch it.

"Touch it" means pounding a fist or foot or knee into a very flimsy fender and not noticing the dent.

Dent, not ding.

They may call out something like "Last one there's a rotten egg!" or "Last one there has to sit by Mom!" or "Last one there looks like Dad!" You want to say, "**Stop it! Stop it! Stop it!** I don't like that game!"

This will guarantee it continues for many, many years.

You may end up with a banged up car, but you'll get some time to yourself if you walk slowly. You'll get even more time if you turn around and run the other way.

Going for Groceries

Getting groceries can be very expensive if you don't have a small-caliber pistol and an old pair of panty hose to pull down over your face.

While you are busy in the produce department—trying to figure out if it's worth it to get a 50-pound sack of B-grade potatoes—your children are pillaging the potato-chip aisle and prefabricated baked-goods display.

You've become distracted by the spuds' gunny sack. Now what could that be used for? Your shroud, maybe? And so you don't see your children lobbing goodies into your cart. Each has been opened and gnawed on.

(This would make a wonderful Disney nature film, but anyone can see it live late in the afternoon in any grocery store.)

Now you can't afford the potatoes and your cart's too full to use the eight-items-or-less checkout lane. You'll be here till breakfast.

At this point

1. Say, "Last one to the car smells like the refrigerator meat tray!"

2. Get a new cart.

Bite-Sized Dinner

Tired of cooking?

No. Really?

Herd the kids over to the store late Friday afternoon and let them graze on the free-sample fiesta. Let them bug some other adults for a while.

Caution: This works only if you convince them to play "We Aren't Related." They ignore you; you ignore them. Fortunately, they *really* enjoy this game.

Dinner with Grandma and Grandpa

Your parents or your spouse's parents might invite your family and all the clan over for a big family meal once in a while.

Be very nice to these old people.

They have **food**.

Their children have all grown up and mo d away.

These people smile a lot and even laugh right out loud.

You're really doing them a favor, bringing over those screaming bottomless pits who call them Grandma and Grandpa. The older generation truly likes to spend a lot of money putting out a first-class spread. "Eat up!" they say.

When it's time to take your children home, their grandparents say, "Our children have all grown up and moved away."

And they smile.

Then they laugh, right out loud.

It'll be a long time before they notice that you took the beef from their freezer and carried it home in your diaper bag.

You might feel guilty if you only take, take, take. So give.

Give them a kid.

Be careful. If you don't hide him well, they might discover him before you back the car out of the driveway.

Take your phone off the hook when you get home.

Less than Kissin' Cousins

When the extended family gets together, brothers and sisters compare their children. You could get caught up in the competition, but it's much easier to just let the cousins beat each other up to see who's the best.

Stay cool when one of your siblings says, "And our little Jerry just got the Peewee Nobel Prize for his science project. And Darlene is waiting to hear the results of her screen test. We think she's ready to leave Broadway for Hollywood."

It doesn't help for you to say, "My little Bubba can reach level seven on Nintendo's 'Super Mario Brothers.'" It's much more effective if you say, "Blood is streaming from Darlene's nose and splashing on her pretty pink pinafore. Jerry's head is stuck in the upstairs commode."

How do you make sure this happens?

Before family gatherings, say to your kids, "I want you to treat your cousins just the way you treat each other. They're family, so the same rules apply."

Three knockdowns are a TKO.

On the Road

As a parent, you know that the journey of a thousand miles begins with one step toward the bathroom.

It's always a mistake to tell your child it's going to be a long trip because this has a devastating effect on the bladder. Then your child, your little baby, will be forced to use a **public restroom.**

For the child's own safety, you must stress:

- Do not sit down.

- Do not lean on anything.

- Do not touch anything.

- Do not look around.

- Do not go in if you have to make boom-boom, only if you have to go wee-wee.

- Do not ask Mommy or Daddy how the never-ending cloth handtowel works or what is in any dispensing machine.

It's important that your child realizes it would be healthier for him to eat carrots grown in a nuclear dump site, or lick the floor at the bus depot, or kiss a game-show host on the lips than to use a public restroom.

Knowing how dangerous and disgusting this place is he'll want to stop at one every three to five miles. Your only chance to ensure his survival is to make him 100 percent phobic about bathroom fixtures.

Read him terrifying fairy tales while he's still young. Substitute "toilet" for witch and "urinal" for wolf.

You just may be saving his life.

Car Games

Maybe you've noticed that your children can entertain themselves in the car for a little while playing things like "I Spit on Your Face," "Car Sick," and "Make a Naughty Gesture at the Big Hairy Men Riding the Motorcycles and Wearing Leather Jackets and Nazi Helmets."

But then the situation may get a little out of hand. You need some other crowd pleasers. Things like "Daddy's Going to Reach Back There and Then You'll Be Sorry," "Don't Say One Word for the

Next Hundred Miles," and "Can You Hold Your Breath Until You Pass Out?"

Offer a **really good** prize so everyone will want to play, something like a remote-control color TV or an 18-speed bicycle or the right to live for another half hour.

Fun for the Whole Family

A little planning goes a long way when it comes to family entertainment. Ask yourself, "What does my family like to do?"

Fight.

That's right. And when is the fighting the best?

When everyone is tired and hungry and can't get away from everyone else.

Right! And where do you get all that and more?

Camping!

Uh-huh! It also costs a lot of money for equipment you don't know how to use; you drive a long way to stay at a campground that's more like a parking lot; and you get to sleep on the ground next to people who drink an amazing amount of alcohol, carry big axes and long knives, and look like they don't like you.

In fact, you **really** make them **angry.**

No wonder your kids love this!

But there's no need to go to all that bother. Just toss sleeping bags out in the back yard, turn on the sprinkler and crawl in. Don't eat for 48 hours, and get an inmate from the nearest prison for the criminally insane to make a surprise visit.

It'll be just like the real McCoy. But no long drive or big gas bill!

Chapter Eight

The winner of the science contest is always the kid whose dad is a rocket scientist and can bring home a baggie of plutonium.

School

Every child must to go to school. If he's at school, he's not home.

Do Not Cooperate

Maybe you're considering a co-op preschool for your 2-, 3-, or 4-year-old. They cost a little less than a regular preschool, but you have to spend one day a week with a dozen children **just like yours**.

It's much safer and more personally rewarding to work part-time or moonlight for extra money to send your child to a regular pre-school. Holding a knife to a cabby's throat and demanding all his cash is a more pleasant and relaxed experience than making sure a dozen tykes don't eat paste or stick popsicle sticks up their noses.

Why Would I Care If They Did?

Why would you care if these little children under your supervision ate several pounds of paste or shoved wooden sticks up their snouts?

Do you mean you **wouldn't** care?

Say, have you ever considered becoming a teacher?

Think about it.

It's OK to Cry

On the day you dropped your child off at preschool maybe you couldn't help bursting into tears as you walked from the classroom. There's no reason to feel embarrassed about this. All parents get teary-eyed when they ask themselves, "Why didn't I do this sooner? What the hell is the matter with me?"

Don't be so hard on yourself.

"Look at That!"

Your preschooler will bring home a...uh...thing that she's very proud of. It's your job to compliment her. You say, "Look at that!"

Don't fall into the trap of saying, "What a pretty picture!" or "Thank you for the glob of dried plaster you mashed your hand into when it was wet and then painted and put a little hanger on the back that **no way on earth** will hold the weight of this manhole cover."

Don't do that because your kid will be bringing home trash throughout her school career and you'd have to adapt your response every time.

"What a nice poem."

"What a good book report."

"What a pretty diploma."

"What a lovely doctorate degree."

No, no, no.

Always: "Look at that!"

Pomp and Circumstantial Evidence

Some gung ho, fruitcake parent whose kid is in your kid's pre-school class is going to insist on a graduation ceremony. You can live with that. You can skip it. But this airhead will also give his or her child a gift and your child will find out about it and then what do you do?

You say, "What a nice idea, honey. I bought you a **savings bond.**"

Remember all the times your parents said they bought you a **savings bond,** or your grandma was sending you a **savings bond,** or everybody else on the block got a bike or a pair of skates or even a wool scarf and you were going to get a **savings bond?**

Have you ever in your life actually seen a **savings bond?**

Case closed.

What Is the Difference Between Preschool and Kindergarten?

It's your job to know this. In preschool the kids glue macaroni to construction paper. In kindergarten, the teacher spray-paints the noodles gold after the kids glue them on the construction paper.

This is part of an ongoing national effort to discourage children from eating or otherwise misusing school supplies. You can help out at home by showing your student how to correctly gnaw on pencils, sniff new books, create lewd pieces of art with paper-clips, and master all the other socially acceptable substitutes adults practice daily.

Private vs. Public Schools

As your child prepares to enter first grade you, for the first time, take a long, hard look at the private and public educational systems and ask yourself, "Which system will **really** stick it to my child?"

A good question. Unfortunately, finances often determine your choice for you. If money is a problem now and will be a problem for the next 12 or 16 years, choose private education. Private school costs between $5,000 and $10,000 a year, but your kid wears a uniform.

Public school is free but your kid wears name-brand clothes.

The List

On the first day of each school year your child comes home with a list of supplies he needs by the next morning. This leaves you very little time to run out and get a second mortgage on the house **and** get to the store. It's much easier if you plan this expense into your budget. You'll have enough money if you don't eat during August.

You'll also notice that the list includes a large box of tissues. This seems a mysterious request since your child has never used a tissue in his life.

These are for his teacher.

Give her a break, huh?

How would you feel if you had to face him every morning and you weren't even **related!**

Standardized Tests

Once a year or so your little girl will be given a standardized test comparing her with other little boys and girls in the same grade across the country.

It would be a big mistake to make sure she got a good night's sleep before the test and had a hearty breakfast that morning. Then she, and you, would have no excuses for her scores.

Fortunately the computer printout of her test results makes no sense to anyone. Tell her you're very proud of her. Tell her you're getting her a **savings bond.**

Parent-Teacher Conferences

A parent-teacher conference is a wonderful opportunity for both parties involved. You and your child's teacher get to sit in the same room for 15 minutes and say, "Where do you suppose he is now?" and "I don't know, but at least neither of us has to worry about him for the next quarter of an hour."

Enjoy the break.

Just for Fun

If you want to have a little fun, stop by your son's school and let him see you talking with his teacher. Check out the look on his face!

It's the same one you have when he walks in the house and says, "Don't believe what the police tell you."

Thank You, Mr. Bus Driver

Maybe your child takes a big, yellow bus to school each day. Notice the driver, how he always has a big smile for every kid, no matter how many climb on board carrying a boom box the size of a three-bedroom ranch house.

Make friends with him.

Find out if you need a prescription for what he has or if you can buy it over the counter.

The Field Trip

If you have a child in school, you'll be asked to drive a car full of kids on a field trip. The schools are pretty darned picky about who drives. The teacher will ask you things like

- "Do you have enough seat belts in your car?"

- "Do you have the right kind of insurance?"

- "Does noise or activity bother you, or have you had a lobotomy?"

These are bad destination choices for a field-trip driver:

- a trout farm

- the art museum

- the ballet

And this is a complete list of all the good choices:

- a brewery

The Room Parent

Your child's teacher will also try to nab you to become a "room parent" (most likely because your child volunteered you in a last-ditch effort to get at least a "D" in conduct and cooperation). Back when you were a student there were only room mothers, but now there's been a social and sexual revolution—too late, you missed it. You were busy rinsing out didies in the toilet—and now dads help out in the classroom too.

Some fathers liked being called *room mothers* and wore a string of pearls and matching earrings just like June Cleaver's, but most objected to the term so now they call you a *room parent*.

Being a room parent involves a lot of work and **no pay**.

But you do get to meet all the kids in your child's class and embarrass him in front of them.

Seriously consider it.

Let the Games Begin

It's also your responsibility to help your child prepare for the annual science-fair competition. But don't get your hopes up. First place always goes to the little kid whose father is a rocket scientist and can bring home a baggie of plutonium as easily as you can steal a box of pencils from your place of employment.

No matter what you do, your child will not win.

The same is true for the cake-decorating contest that's part of the school's annual bazaar. No matter how many pounds of coconut you dye green to look like grass or how many lemon drops you use to make a sun, an eight-foot, spun-sugar Taj Mahal will take the gold medal.

Your kid won't do well in the speech contest either, but at least in this case you can get him in trouble, especially if he's in first or second grade. Have him stand up straight and shout out when he begins, "There once was a man from Nantucket..." or "There was a young lady from Venus...."

Let's Hear It for the Band

The school band is one of those gray areas. If your kid joins, you can pester him to practice every day, but he just may double-cross you and practice every day.

Then there's the semiannual concert where you're stuck in a school auditorium listening to students play **Maim That Tune!** What is that they're playing, anyway? Let us help you. It's either "Ode to Joy," "Downtown," or "Louie, Louie."

In this case it's really worth your while to own a video camera. Parents who have shelled out a thousand dollars on a minicam get to stand up and walk around. After you've spent seven or eight hours on a metal folding chair a thousand dollars doesn't sound like very much money.

It sounds like a bargain.

A New Age

Video equipment has changed the classroom forever. Your child probably sees a movie at least once a week and has yet to see the two you saw every year when you were in school: *The Blasting Cap: Now They Call Him "Lefty"* and *Duck and Cover It and Kiss It Goodbye.*

No, they see things like *Babysitter Zombie* and *Prom Queen of Slaughterhouse High.*

What? You didn't know that!

Hold on. Before you go after your child's teacher, realize that in each bloody horror flick some little kid who sasses his parents and his teacher always has his heart ripped out before the end of the movie.

In other words, it's educational.

Report Cards

You'd better hope your little one learns more than that lippy kids get their lungs pulled out through their noses. That's an important lesson, but it's not one of the subjects graded on a report card.

You probably need very little help when it comes to looking at your child's report card. After all, you watched what your parents did all those years:

1. Sputter

2. Gasp

3. Threaten

4. Sign it

Do **not** let your child know you wish you'd gotten grades that high when you were in school.

Do **not** let your child talk to your parents or brothers or sisters near report-card time.

The VCR at Home

A video cassette recorder can help you get your child out of the sack on a wintry school day. Simply tape Saturday morning cartoons and replay them—nice and loud—first thing on a school morning.

Stand back so you aren't trampled by your child charging toward the TV set.

Surprise! It isn't really Saturday!

Choosing a Profession

Give the same tape to your child's spouse so he or she can use it to help get your kid to work on time. And what kind of work **will** he be doing?

Let's see....

Your child's not doing well in his studies, he doesn't get along well with the others, and his teacher is really honked off at him all the time.

That's right, he's following in **your** footsteps.

Tell him that. Tell him he's going to end up **just like you.**

He'll find that more frightening than the babysitter zombie or prom queen of Slaughterhouse High turning his way and licking her chops.

Don't razz him if he starts sleeping with a light on.

Chapter Nine

Tell her to wait by the flagpole. Make sure she has her sleeping bag and toothbrush.

After School

It seems to hurt more if you hit yourself in the head with a brick for a long, long time, stop for a few minutes, and then begin again.

It feels the same to see your child walk into the house after school.

How to Keep Your Child Out

You can keep your child outside the house. Tactics vary according to age.

- Kindergarten to third grade: don't answer the doorbell.

- Fourth to sixth grade: in the middle of a school day, change the locks.

- Junior high: in the middle of a school day, move to a different country.

- High school: tape your VISA card to the front door.

A Better Plan

Of course, it's much easier and less expensive if you can make sure your child has to stay after school.

- Put a pack of cigarettes in her lunch sack so it will fall out in the middle of class when she tries to sneak a sour cream-green onion potato chip.

- Call the school with a bomb threat and use her name.

- Force the dog to eat her homework and advise her to just tell the teacher the simple truth.

Extracurricular Activities

Yes, at your school "extracurricular activities" meant stealing the vice principal's hubcaps or teasing your hair or blowing spit bubbles, but we're talking about things like band, debate, drama, chess club, wrestling, and so on.

Remember how often your parents bent your ear trying to get you involved in some activity like this? To stay late and have some fun?

Now you know why.

"Wait by the Flagpole"

There's not much you can do to keep your child after school if he's still in the primary grades, except tell him he can't ride the bus because you'll be picking him up. Tell him to wait by the flagpole. Make sure he has a sleeping bag and toothbrush.

Help Your Child Be a Sport

Sooner or later your kid is going to show up at home, and it will be bad news for you if you are not prepared.

So get him involved in sports. Tell him you're sure he can be a professional athlete and star in deodorant commercials.

Sports change with the seasons, but there are enough of them to keep him busy all year long.

Be sure to have his equipment ready as soon as he walks in the door so you can very helpfully say, **"Don't sit down! Here! Goodbye!"**

That sounds a little cold, doesn't it?

Why not add, "Work hard, Son! Someday your armpits will be known across the country!"

Give him a goal!

Be sure to remind your child that it isn't important if the team wins or loses, or how much playing time he gets, or how well he does. What's important is that practices and games are not held at your house.

Let's Try Something!

Try to interest your child in the Boy Scouts, Girl Scouts, Camp Fire Girls, or some other worthwhile group in which he or she will learn to take orders without talking back. There's no better way to prepare a youngster for the adult world, whether your child is headed for prison or marriage or both.

Doin' Chores

Having your child perform simple, helpful tasks around the house is another way to teach him responsibility. You can begin when he is very young, like about three hours old. You can say, "Son, I'd like you to mow the lawn."

You'll get the same results when your son is 16.

Keep calling them **chores** on the miniscule chance your child might not realize you mean **work.** Chores sound like something the little kid on "Lassie" would do. Or something Hoss on "Bonanza" had to do before he could ride into town and blush at some babe you knew he wasn't going to marry because on Saturday morning he couldn't be at any fool wedding—he had chores to do.

The Startling Truth

We hate to bring this up, but the sad fact is that television shows are not like real life.

Sure, you say, but isn't TV more realistic today?

Some of it is. We're not talking about made-for-TV movies where a fourth-grader sends a penny to a record club, is named co-conspirator in a major drug ring, is falsely convicted and sent to a federal prison where he learns to play the banjo, and then 84 years later two very attractive law students study the case and say, "Hey, there's been a miscarriage of justice here," and on and on and on until the final scene where Mickey Rooney is flanked by the two students who sprung him and they're all singing "Oh! Susanna."

TV movies are much more realistic than weekly sitcoms about family life. On these programs both parents and children say very witty things. You know very well the wittiest exchange at your home has been "Shut up" and "Make me."

But **keep watching these shows!** And notice that in each episode there's one scene where the parents cling to each other in a corner and say, "It's us against them."

You can't get more real than that.

Afternoon TV

Programmers at local television stations try to help you out by running classic shows between the time school gets out and dinner time. They have kids, too.

You may hope that your kids will see what a swell guy Mr. Anderson is and what a darling Mrs. Brady is, but it's a long shot.

You can quiz your child at dinner with questions like, "Well, did Bud Anderson get that old jalopy running?" But **do not** be upset when the answer is, "If transvestites get married in Connecticut only one can wear a wedding gown and it can't be white."

Reruns on local stations may be popular with parents like you, but your children are watching network TV talk shows.

But Not Until...

You *can't* allow your child to watch any television until her homework is done. You know this. So check to make sure she's completed all her assignments:

You: Have you finished your homework?

Her: Yeah.

You: OK.

We know, we know. Sometimes it just doesn't happen that way. Sometimes it's like this:

You: Have you finished your homework?

Her: I ain't got none.

You: OK.

Then make her switch channels from the panel of superior court judges who are married to a variety of fresh vegetables and sit down with her to enjoy the last half of "The Jetsons."

Doesn't My Child Need My Help?

What's that? Doesn't your child need your help to do her homework?

No, she needs somebody who could do it correctly.

That pretty much leaves you out, huh?

If you try to help her, she'll get mad because she doesn't understand it, and you'll get mad because you don't understand it. You'll find out how little she really knows, but she'll know that you don't know very much yourself. In fact, she'll know you're pretty darned stupid. And who's going to fix dinner? You'll have to phone for a pizza and both of you will be too upset to enjoy it.

That's no good for either of you.

So skip right to the pizza part.

And speaking of skipping, hold the green peppers.

How about that geeky little judge who wasn't even married to that bell pepper but was just living with it?

Some people have no moral code.

Working Outside the Home

Most likely you didn't just win $8 billion in the state lottery so you have to work outside the home, and your child heads for a day-care center or a baby-sitter directly from school.

Some parents worry because their day-care operator is not a Green Beret. Don't be concerned. A former army ranger or professional wrestler does just as well.

Summer, a Bummer

Your child will be home for **three months** unless she does poorly in class and has to go to summer school.

Get it?

OK. But let's say you mess up and your child passes and she's going to be home for 90 days.

Sounds like a Stephen King novel.

Why not just say, "I'm glad I have this opportunity. Quality time never seemed to work and now my child and I can spend quantity time with each other. This is going to be the best summer ever! Camping, hiking, picnics, the book club at the library, movies, day trips, a nice family vacation, paint the house.... This is going to be great!"

Then stop off at a sporting goods shop and buy a tranquilizer gun. No, don't aim that weapon at your child! What's the **matter** with you, anyway? You can't hit a moving target with your hands shaking the way they are.

Shoot yourself.

Chapter Ten

How to keep your child in bed at night.

Go to Bed!

Maybe you're asking, "Why does this book have an entire chapter on getting a child to go to bed?"

We reply, "Welcome to planet Earth."

The Danger of Bonding

Remember when your child was born and you wanted to be close to him and hold him and hug him and do all those little things that are "bonding"?

You made a **big** mistake.

Bonding means your child knows what you really want. He can tell when you're totally exhausted and about to collapse. That's why, when you say, "It's nappy time," he defecates in his diapers.

And giggles.

For his own health and well-being, he needs to be on a strict daily schedule.

Sign him up at a monastery.

Classic Techniques

Your infant's internal clock is as precise as a $1.98 digital watch (with a $1 mail-in rebate). It's not surprising, then, that she doesn't know or care if it's day or night. She only knows how to eat, burp, poop, sleep, and try to ignore that giant creature who keeps sobbing. She may take 10 minutes or 10 weeks to accomplish all these tasks.

Ten minutes one time and 10 weeks the next.

That's why you must gradually adjust your newborn to your schedule. It will seem like a long, long time but in only four or five years the two of you will be perfectly synchronized.

You'll match her perfectly.

The Lessons of War

Historians tell us of a brainwashing method perfected during the Korean War. A POW was handed an infant and in no time at all that strapping young soldier had all the will, drive, and verve of Silly Putty.

International law has since made this technique illegal.

Saturation bombing is one thing, but babies....

This explains why you don't think twice about eating the remains of a soggy sandwich a three-year-old has sucked on for an hour, why you fall asleep brushing your teeth, and why you laugh so heartily at the Count on "Sesame Street."

How can you avoid being brainwashed?

Easy.

Don't have kids.

Oh, sorry, too late. In that case, keep reminding yourself, "I am not going crazy. I'm just thinking and acting as if I have."

Instructions for the Baby-sitter

You need to get out more. You and your spouse should go out to dinner. Have an adult evening.

Use forks.

That means tonight you don't have to worry about putting your baby to bed. The baby-sitter will do that.

Let's say you've found a really great sitter at a reasonable price. You haven't, but let's say it.

Here's how to have a night on the town:

1. You and your spouse stay awake long enough to get dressed up.
2. The baby-sitter shows up.
3. You pick up the baby to kiss him goodbye.
4. You change your clothes.
5. You tell the baby-sitter bedtime is 7:30.
6. She asks if there are any Ding Dongs in the house.
7. You and your spouse drive to a nice restaurant where the wait will only be an hour or so.
8. You go to McDonald's instead and burst into tears when you see the Happy Meal boxes, which remind you of your baby.
9. You feel bad that you miss your baby.
10. You feel bad about feeling bad about missing your baby.
11. You eat quickly.
12. Your spouse nods off and ends up facedown in a McD.L.T. Good thing it's the cool side.

13. You drive home.

14. You walk in the house, knowing your baby has missed you as much as you missed him.

15. Your baby wakes up.

16. It's 7:25.

17. There are no more Ding Dongs in the house.

Don't worry about following this plan exactly. You can substitute with a Filet-O-Fish sandwich and Twinkies if you prefer.

But Most of the Time

You can't expect to have a big night out very often. Most of the time you'll be the one putting your child in the sack.

It seems cruel, but we agree with those who advise that if your baby cries when she's put down for bed, you should ignore her.

She ignores **your** blubbering, doesn't she?

Busy yourself with something else and she'll soon be asleep. Fighting with your spouse over whether you should rush back into the nursery and pick her up is always a good choice.

Let 'Em Vent

There's a big difference between getting an infant to sleep at night and trying to do the same thing with a little older child.

The infant cries and fusses for hours and hours.

The child does the same **and** tells you how much he hates you.

If you have an older child, let him vent his anger. Let him know it's OK with you if he does.

Say, "I don't care."

"I'm Thirsty!"

"I want a drink of water!" is one of the most common ploys a child uses to stay up a little—or a lot—past his bedtime.

You can handle this easily if you choose the right bedtime book to read to your child. We recommend the U.S. surgeon general's report on the chemical contamination of the public water supply.

And maybe a little something about communism and fluoride.

Don't Surprise Your Child

Give your child ample warning that she has to go to bed.

Say, "Come on, come on, come on, let's move it, huh? Rise and shine and don't forget you have to go to bed in 14 hours."

Pull the covers off her if she still doesn't get up. Tell her that her brother is devouring all the cold, leftover pizza and she'll have to eat oatmeal for breakfast if she doesn't hustle.

A Monster in the Closet

Quite often a child will say he's afraid to go to bed because there's a monster in his closet. You must realize that he is truly frightened.

Tuck him into bed, then open the closet door and show him there's no monster in there.

Then give him a good-night kiss and tell him the monster is **under his bed**, and it will **grab him by the ankle** if he tries to step out of bed and will **drag him under and keep him there for all eternity.**

Leave the door open a little and the hall light on.

Is that Enough?

"Is that really enough to keep my child in bed?" you may be asking.

Maybe not.

If you have any doubts, before leaving the room peek under the bed and say, "Good night, monster. My, you look hungry!"

Going Potty

The monster method will work until your child learns to clamber over the dresser or jump all the way from the bed to the hallway.

Why would he do this?

He's gotta go potty.

It could be worse. He could stay in bed.

Remember that it takes a while for your child to get ready to hit the hay. You need to give him enough time. Say, "Finish your lunch. Good night."

Putting on the Brakes

Your job will be a lot easier if you calm your child with a series of activities in the evening. You can't expect someone to drop right off after running on a Nintendo pad for six hours and watching kids her age on "Double Dare" slide through Dutch chocolate pudding. Try this:

"Let's turn off the TV now and play a little game before bedtime, honey. Let's pretend we're very sick. Good! Now let's pretend we're dying. Atta girl! And now we're dead. Shhh. Now we're going to play 'Cemetery.'"

Who Are You Kidding?

But those games probably won't work, will they? And why not? Because they begin with you saying "Let's turn off the TV."

We hate to keep harping on the same old tune, but, once again, we suggest you rely on your VCR. What you really need to say is "Let's tape this show so we can fast-forward the commercials. In the meantime, let's play a little game...."

Keep Lots of Cassettes on Hand

The same approach works when it's past your child's bedtime and she shrieks that she wants to see the end of a show. Don't you wish you had a nickel for every time this happened in your home?

You: Darling, it's two hours past your bedtime.

Her: Quiet! I wanna see if J.R. is the father.

You: That's no excuse, honey. Besides, you know he can't have children after that run-in with the rabid armadillo.

Her: Oh, yeah.

You: So nighty-night.

Her: Look! He's putting an armadillo in that young woman's panty hose drawer.

This is when you say: "I'll tape it."

What Happened to Reverse Psychology?

Hey, you may be saying about now, didn't this book recommend forcing a child to stay up late if he was naughty?

Us: We said that?

You: In the first chapter.

Us: Did you read all the way from Chapter 1 or have you been skipping around?

You: Skipping around.

Us: In that case, we explained that apparent discrepancy several chapters ago. We're embarrassed for you that you even brought it up.

OK, But at the Next Commercial

Never tell your child he can stay up until the next commercial.

You won't believe how long that will take. Suddenly the television networks don't want to make any money.

We would warn you to especially avoid saying this if you were watching a public television station with your child. But there's no need for that, is there?

New Pajamas

You've probably noticed that your child needs new pajamas every day because he's outgrown the pair he wore the night before.

Even in his sleep—he nodded off for about 15 minutes last night but you missed it because you had already passed out—his body continues to get bigger.

All too soon he will be **bigger than you are!**

Keep in mind that you can never rely on strength alone because a day will come when he's stronger than you.

But you can always be **more** devious.

Chapter Eleven

Hire some video-arcade punks to supervise the games at your house.

Sibling Rivalry, Civil War

A **sibling** is someone who has the same mother or father as you and thinks you're about as smart as bread mold. But mold dresses better and is more fun at parties.

Don't get the idea that kids in the same family have always fought with each other. Only since Cain killed Abel.

But this doesn't have to happen in your house.

Unless you have more than one child.

If you do, tell them they're not related. Tell each one separately that the other one is a neighbor kid.

A child is always nicer to a neighbor kid than to a brother or sister.

Rank in the Family

The oldest child in any family was an only child at one time. That's why oldest children are so snotty. Even after they're adults. You've probably noticed this.

The youngest child is always the baby of the family. That's why youngest children are so snotty. Even after they're adults. You've probably noticed this.

Middle children were never the oldest and were the baby for only a short time. They think they're better than the oldest and the baby. This is why they're so snotty. Even after they're adults. You've probably noticed this.

This doesn't have to be a problem with your children. It will always be this way, but you can just quit noticing it.

Money, Money, Money

It's a really big mistake to have more than one child and not be stinking, filthy rich, even though it's not possible to have more than one child and be stinking, filthy rich. But if you have an only child, you run the risk of having a namby-pamby, spoiled miniature adult who beats you at cribbage and tells you to clean your room.

Choose poverty.

Preparing for a Baby Brother or Sister

It's wise to prepare your child for the coming of a new brother or sister. Buy her a baby doll and let her beat the hell out of that.

Maybe then she'll leave the new baby alone.

Helping Mommy and Daddy

An older child will want to help Mommy and Daddy with the new baby. He'll get mad at it, yell at it, complain about it, and wish Mr. Stork had dropped this bundle of trouble on somebody else's doorstep.

In other words, he'll act just like Mommy and Daddy.

That's the last thing you need.

Instead, buy your child a pet he can hate taking care of.

Almost Twins

As your children get a little older, you can dress them in matching outfits. Take a lot of pictures of them because even 30, 40, or 50 years later your kids will still hate being reminded of it.

"Baby! Baby! Baby!"

Your older child probably teases your younger one. He makes fun of her and says mean things like "You don't got any teeth!" "You don't got any hair!"

Don't bother trying to stop him.

Let your younger child learn these phrases.

She can use them a little later when she greets her brother at family reunions.

Be Fair

It's important that you don't play favorites. For example, it would be really crass to let only one of your children take kick-boxing lessons. Unless the other one had some teeth that were about to come out anyway.

"I Did My Half!"

If you ask two of your children to clean a bedroom they share, each will immediately reply, "I did my half!"

Obviously they've chosen the ceiling half, not the floor half. And you have to admit, except for that single banana slice, the ceiling looks pretty darned good.

So how do you get them to clean their bedroom?

You can't. But parents have discovered that yelling at their kids gets their hearts thumping and lungs pumping. In today's lingo, it's aerobic. You'll enjoy the exercise even more if you realize the room will never be clean and the whole point is for you to have a 20-minute "At Least Pick Up Your Socks and Underwear" workout.

Three times a week.

Wouldn't This Work?

You may be asking, "Wouldn't it work to give each child his or her own bedroom?"

No.

Then your child will say she didn't mess it up. It was her brother who came in there and wrecked everything.

Tell your child she has to stay in there until it is all cleaned up. And shut the door.

She won't come out for 10 or 15 minutes. The room may look the same, but you've had 10 or 15 minutes of quiet.

Unless, of course, you had to spend the whole time arguing with her brother about his room.

Put It Away

Maybe sometimes two of your children fight over the same toy.

Wow! That's never happened in any other family. What kind of a parent are you?

One says, "It's mine!" and the other cleverly argues, "It's mine!" and then they both say, "I had it first!" After they've been at it for an hour or so, try this: "It's time to clean up."

Then one will say, "It's not mine. It's his." And the other will say, "He had it last." And the fight will continue for another hour.

It won't be any quieter, but at least it'll be a new fight.

Or, if your kids aren't screwy enough already, keep telling them, "Put it away!" and then, "Never mind. You can keep playing!" and watch them try to adjust.

By Any Other Name

We know it's hard for you to yell at your children because you keep calling them the wrong name. Then they laugh at how stu pid you are and you get madder.

It was funny when your mom or dad did that with you and your brother or sister but it isn't funny anymore.

Not even a little bit.

So use nicknames. Not a particular nickname for a particular kid. Call any kid any of these names at any time.

- Dead Meat

- Ace

- Bozo

- Kid

- Hey, you. Yeah, YOU!

Life's Not Fair

Your child: "IT'S NOT FAIR!"

You: "Life isn't suppose to be fair."

Save Your Breath

You're aging fast enough. At an alarming rate, in fact. So don't increase it by asking your children any of these **seven really stupid questions.**

1. "Who left the milk out?"

2. "Whose turn is it to set the table?"

3. "Did anybody feed the dog?"

4. "Are the dishes in the dishwasher clean or dirty?"

5. "Did I already give you your allowance?"

6. "Could somebody get the other sack of groceries out of the car?"

7. "Didn't the cat used to have a head?"

Working Together

Your children would never agree on anything if they didn't have a common enemy. They do.

You.

Your job as a parent may not be easier to perform, but it will be easier to understand if you watch a lot of prison movies. You'll realize that your children are planning how to get you 24 hours a day.

Which is exactly what they do.

An Ancient Plan

Strangely enough, it's to your advantage to stop your children from cooperating with one another.

Divide and conquer?

No.

More like, divide and possibly survive.

You need to say things about one child that really **irritate** the other.

- "Your brother was a big help to me today. He took out the garbage without anyone even asking him."

- "Your sister was so good about doing her homework. Why can't you be more like her?"

- "I don't think a parent should play favorites. But that brother of yours...."

It's better to stick with comments like the last example. You have to take out the garbage or do your daughter's homework to use number one or two.

For More Fun!

For a great variation on how to divide and survive, take the garbage out yourself when no one is looking. Then at dinner say, "I want to thank a certain person for being so nice to me and taking the garbage out without my asking. I really appreciate it. I'm not going to name names, but that person knows who I'm talking about. Thank you so very much. I just wish your brothers and sisters were more like you."

Make sure whoever sets the table that evening—probably you, right?—doesn't put any sharp knives out.

Video-Game Mania

You can spend $100 for a video-game machine and then $20 to $30 for each game cartridge so your children can sit on the living room floor and bicker over who made the other mess up.

The manufacturers will tell you that playing a home version is the same as playing in a video arcade. This is not true.

Little children like yours do not fight with each other in the arcade because there are older children there—children with cigarettes and tattoos and three-day's beard stubble—who politely tell them, "Shut up, punk."

Video-game playing will go much more smoothly in your home if you rent one of these fine young gentlemen to supervise. The cost can easily be offset if you charge your child 25 cents for each game he or she plays.

The Multi-TV Family

When you were a kid you and your brothers and sisters fought over what television show to watch. Thanks to modern technology, the low cost of electronics, and your greedy buy-buy-buy, charge-charge-charge mentality, that's no longer a problem.

Your children can each watch a separate show at the same time. They only fight over which set they get to use.

Isn't it sad the way your littlest kid is always stuck in the back bedroom watching the old black-and-white with the coat-hanger antenna? Too bad for her.

But you can brighten up your day by playing "Hide the Remote." The child who ended up with the big-screen TV in the living room will practically die because he has to get up and turn the set on and can't bounce from channel to channel during commercials.

A Lovely Gift

Ah, what the heck. Give the remote to the little kid stuck with the black-and-white set—it won't work, but just holding it makes her feel powerful. Tell her you yelled at her big brother for losing it.

But do this only on her birthday.

The Ultimate Goal

A trick like that—being nice—can really confuse your child and that's your ultimate goal. It's more difficult for a confused child to plot against you. That's why this, our last piece of advice, works so well.

Wrap your arms around your child and say, "I love you."

It never fails.

How to Survive Your 40th Birthday
by Bill Dodds

Bill Dodds shows those reaching middle age that there's more to life after 40, namely old age and death. This book offers outrageous advice to those facing the bleak future, including how to act surprised at your 40th birthday party.

Order # 4260

Dads Say the Dumbest Things!
by Bruce Lansky and K.L. Jones

Lansky and Jones have collected all of the greatest lines dads have ever used to get kids to stop fighting in the car, feed the pet, turn off the TV while doing their homework, and get home before curfew. It includes such winners as: "What do you want a pet for—you've got a sister" and, "When I said 'feed the goldfish,' I didn't mean feed them to the cat." A fun gift for dad.

Order #4220

Moms Say the Funniest Things!
by Bruce Lansky

Bruce Lansky has collected the greatest lines moms have ever used to deal with "emergencies" like getting the kids out of bed in the morning, cleaned, dressed, to school, to the dinner table, undressed, and back to bed. It includes such all-time winners as: "Put on clean underwear—you never know when you'll be in an accident" and, "If God had wanted you to fool around, He would have written the 'Ten Suggestions.'" A fun gift for mom.

Order #4280

How To Embarrass Your Kids Without Even Trying

by Joan Holleman and Audrey Sherins

When kids hit the preteen years, just about everything their parents do embarrasses them. This book lists over 600 ways parents can drive their kids up the wall. . . without even trying.

Order #4005

Grandma Knows Best, But No One Ever Listens!

by Mary McBride

Mary McBride offers much-needed advice for new grandmas on how to:

- Show baby photos to anyone, any time
- Get out of babysitting . . . or if stuck, to housebreak the kids before they wreck the house
- Advise the daughter-in-law without being banned from her home

A perfect gift for grandma, Phyllis Diller says it's "harder to put down than a new grandchild."

Order #4009

Kids Pick the Funniest Poems

compiled by Bruce Lansky

Three hundred elementary kids will tell you that this book contains the funniest poems for kids because they picked them! Not surprisingly, they chose many of the funniest poems ever written by favorites like Dr. Seuss, Shel Silverstein, Jack Prelutsky, Jeff Moss, and Judith Viorst. Plus poems by lesser known writers that are just as funny. This book is guaranteed to please children ages 6–12!

Order #2410

Order Form

Qty	Title	Author	Order #	Price	Total
	Dads Say the Dumbest Things!	Lansky/Jones	4220	$6.00	
	David, We're Pregnant!	Johnston, L.	1049	$6.00	
	Do They Ever Grow Up?	Johnston, L.	1089	$6.00	
	Grandma Knows Best	McBride, M.	4009	$6.00	
	Hi, Mom! Hi, Dad!	Johnston, L.	1139	$6.00	
	How to Embarrass Your Kids	Holleman, Sherins	4005	$6.00	
	How to Outsmart Your Kids	Dodds, B.	4090	$6.00	
	How to Survive Your 40th Birthday	Dodds, B.	4260	$6.00	
	Italian Without Words	Cangelosi/Carpini	5100	$5.00	
	Kids Pick the Funniest Poems	Lansky, B.	2410	$14.00	
	Moms Say the Funniest Things!	Lansky, B.	4280	$6.00	
	Mother Murphy's Law	Lansky, B.	1149	$4.50	
	Mother Murphy's 2nd Law	Lansky, B.	4010	$4.50	
	Papal Bull	Sullivan, D.	4060	$4.95	
	Weird Wonders, Bizarre Blunders	Schreiber, B.	4120	$4.95	
	World's Funniest Roast Jokes	Stangland, R.	4030	$6.00	
	"I Embarrass My Kids Without Even Trying!" Button		4006	$1.00	
				Subtotal	
			Shipping & Handling		
		MN residents add 6.5% sales tax			
				Total	

YES! Please send me the books indicated above. Add $2.00 shipping and handling for the first book and 50¢ for each additional book (no additional charges, however, for button orders). Add $2.50 to total for books shipped to Canada. Overseas postage will be billed. Allow up to 4 weeks for delivery. Send check or money order payable to Meadowbrook Press. No cash or C.O.D.'s, please. Prices subject to change without notice. **Quantity discounts available upon request.**

Send book(s) to:

Name _____ Address _____

City _____ State _____ Zip _____

Telephone (____)_____ P.O. number (if necessary) _____

Payment via: ❏ Check or money order payable to Meadowbrook Press (No cash or C.O.D.'s, please) Amount enclosed $ _____ ❏ Visa (for orders over $10.00 only.)
❏ MasterCard (for orders over $10.00 only.)

Account # _____ Signature _____ Exp. Date _____

A _FREE_ Meadowbrook Press catalog is available upon request.
You can also phone us for orders of $10.00 or more at 1-800-338-2232.

Mail to: Meadowbrook, Inc.
18318 Minnetonka Boulevard, Deephaven, MN 55391
(612) 473-5400   Toll-Free 1-800-338-2232   Fax (612) 475-0736